FRANKFURT TRAVEL GUIDE

2023

A Traveler's Delight Guide into Germany's
Financial Hub

Charles E. Stokes

TABLE OF CONTENTS

4

WELCOME TO FRANKFURT

I was filled with excitement as I left for Frankfurt, Germany, on my first vacation. I was eager to discover the bustling city's feeling of mystery and adventure. It is known for its rich history and lively culture.

As soon as I went onto the streets of Frankfurt after arriving there, the city's dynamic energy welcomed me. It was stunning to see the enormous towers against the clear sky. I was enamored by the city's distinctive fusion of contemporary architecture and old-world charm, and I couldn't help but feel in awe of it.

I traveled to Frankfurt's famous Altstadt, the old town, to fully immerse myself in its history. I was taken back in time by the winding cobblestone lanes that were dotted with historic half-timbered homes and inviting cafes. I came across the majestic Römer, the city hall that has stood proudly for more than six centuries, as I was meandering through the little passageways. I was in awe of its beautiful construction and vivid colors.

I was drawn to the lively market square by the sounds of music and laughing, where sellers were selling a wide variety of regional specialties. The air was filled with the mouthwatering fragrance of bratwurst and pretzels, teasing my taste receptors. I couldn't help myself and indulged in the authentic German food, enjoying each bite and taking in the bustling environment.

I crossed the River Main with a map in hand to explore the incredible Museumsufer, a cluster of top-notch museums along the riverfront. The treasures on exhibit in the Städel Museum mesmerized me as a lover of art. The museum was a voyage through art history that left me inspired and in amazement, featuring everything from Renaissance masterpieces to modern artwork.

I traveled to the recognizable Main Tower to see Frankfurt's contemporary side. I was astounded by the panoramic view of the city when the elevator carried me to the observation deck. Skyscrapers reached the skies, displaying the city's might in business. I couldn't help but appreciate Frankfurt's vibrant energy as the scene brought back memories of Frankfurt's prominence as a major worldwide financial center.

The River Main's banks, where a thriving nightlife awaited, called to me as the sun sank. The lively pubs and clubs were filled with residents and visitors mixing and the city was alive with music, laughing, and the clinking of glasses. I took part in the celebrations, swaying to the music, making new friends, and making memories that would last a lifetime.

My initial visit to Frankfurt well surpassed my expectations. The city's flawless fusion of technology and history, it's kind and inviting environment, and its thriving cultural scene made an enduring impression on my heart. I knew that I would keep a bit of Frankfurt with me as I said goodbye to this fascinating city, cherishing the memories and anxiously anticipating my next journey.

Geography and Climate

Frankfurt is a city known for its vibrant economy, rich cultural heritage, and diverse population. The geography and climate of Frankfurt play significant roles in shaping the city's character and lifestyle.

Geographically, Frankfurt is situated on the banks of the River Main, which divides the city into two parts: the northern part, known as the "Right Bank," and the southern part, known as the "Left Bank." The cityscape is characterized by a mix of historic architecture and modern skyscrapers, earning it the nickname "Mainhattan" due to its resemblance to Manhattan's skyline.

The surrounding region of Frankfurt is relatively flat, with low-lying areas and gently rolling hills. The city itself sits at an elevation of approximately 96 meters (315 feet) above sea level. The fertile plains surrounding Frankfurt make it an important agricultural center, known for its vineyards, orchards, and vegetable farms.

When it comes to climate, Frankfurt experiences a temperate seasonal climate with moderate rainfall throughout the year. Summers in Frankfurt are generally warm and humid, with average temperatures ranging from 20°C to 25°C (68°F to 77°F). It is not uncommon for temperatures to exceed 30°C (86°F) during heatwaves. However, summer evenings tend to cool down, providing some relief from the daytime heat.

Winters in Frankfurt are relatively mild, with average temperatures ranging from 0°C to 5°C (32°F to 41°F). Snowfall is not as common compared to other parts of Germany, but when it does occur, it adds a picturesque touch to the city's landscape. The transition seasons of spring and autumn are characterized by mild temperatures and can be quite pleasant, with blooming flowers in spring and colorful foliage in autumn.

Rainfall in Frankfurt is fairly evenly distributed throughout the year, with no distinct dry season. The city receives an average annual precipitation of around 650 millimeters (25.6 inches). July tends to be the wettest month, while February is usually the driest. The River Main plays a significant role in the city's climate, as it helps moderate temperatures and influences the local weather patterns.

The geography and climate of Frankfurt contribute to its diverse landscape and appealing weather conditions. The city's location on the River Main, combined with its flat surroundings and temperate seasonal climate, make it an attractive destination for both residents and visitors alike. Whether it's enjoying a summer stroll along the riverbanks or witnessing the colorful transformation of the city during autumn, Frankfurt offers a range of experiences influenced by its geographical and climatic characteristics.

Culture and People

Frankfurt is well known for its varied population and rich cultural legacy. Frankfurt, one of Europe's main financial capitals, draws individuals from all walks of life, resulting in a cultural mash-up that adds to the city's distinctive personality.

Frankfurt's culture is a fusion of old-world German traditions with a contemporary, global way of life. The architecture, museums, and festivals of the city reflect its pride in its lengthy past. The Römer, a collection of medieval structures in the heart of the city, is a well-liked tourist destination and a representation of Frankfurt's cultural history. Skyscrapers that tower above the city's landscape serve as a visual representation of its modernity and might.

Frankfurters are the locals who call Frankfurt home and are renowned for being kind and open-minded. The multicultural environment of the city encourages acceptance and tolerance among its citizens. Frankfurt has a wide variety of cuisines, languages, and customs, which reflect this. Frankfurt's culinary culture is an authentic representation of its multiculturalism, ranging from regional specialties from all over the world to typical German meals like bratwurst and sauerkraut.

Frankfurt also holds several cultural occasions and festivals all year long. One of the biggest book fairs in the world, the Frankfurt Book Fair draws writers, publishers, and book enthusiasts from all over the world. Numerous museums along the Main River provide unique exhibitions and concerts as part of the Museum Embankment Festival, which honors art, music, and dance. The Frankfurt Weihnachtsmarkt, or Christmas market, is a beloved custom where locals and visitors meet to enjoy festive decorations, delectable foods, and one-of-a-kind presents.

The abundance of museums and galleries in the city demonstrates its dedication to the arts. The Städel Museum is home to a sizable collection of European artwork that spans the medieval era to modern pieces. The Senckenberg Natural History Museum provides insights into the natural world, while the Museum of Modern Art (MMK) exhibits cutting-edge contemporary art.

Frankfurt places high importance on education and intellectual activities. Several renowned universities, including Goethe University and the Frankfurt University of Applied Sciences, are located in the city. These schools draw students from all around the world, which enhances the city's scholarly and intellectual culture.

Frankfurt is a city that values variety and modernity while preserving its rich cultural past. Frankfurters are kind and accepting, fostering a lively environment where many cultures cohabit together. Frankfurt provides a remarkable fusion of history and innovation that continues to draw tourists from near and far, from its historical sites and museums to its varied cuisine and energetic festivals.

CHAPTER 1: PLANNING YOUR TRIP TO FRANKFURT

Best Time to Visit Frankfurt

The best time to visit Frankfurt largely depends on your preferences and the type of experience you seek. Frankfurt, located in the heart of Germany, experiences a temperate climate with distinct seasons throughout the year. Each season offers its own unique charm and opportunities for exploration.

Spring (March to May) is a delightful time to visit Frankfurt. The city comes alive with vibrant blossoms, and the pleasant weather invites outdoor activities. The average temperatures range from 10°C to 20°C (50°F to 68°F), making it perfect for strolling through the city's picturesque parks and gardens. The famous Palmengarten is particularly enchanting during this time, with its colorful displays of flowers and trees in full bloom.

Summer (June to August) is the peak tourist season in Frankfurt. The weather is warm, with temperatures averaging between 20°C and 25°C (68°F and 77°F). This is a great time to explore the city's numerous festivals and events, such as the Museumsuferfest, which celebrates the city's vibrant arts scene along the banks of the River Main. However, be prepared for larger crowds and higher prices during this period.

Autumn (September to November) brings cooler temperatures to Frankfurt, ranging from 10°C to 20°C (50°F to 68°F). The city's parks and forests transform into a beautiful tapestry of autumn colors, offering breathtaking scenery for nature enthusiasts. The Frankfurt Book Fair, one of the largest book fairs in the world, also takes place in October, attracting book lovers and industry professionals from around the globe.

Winter (December to February) is a quieter time to visit Frankfurt, with fewer tourists. The temperatures can drop to around freezing point, and occasional snowfall adds a magical touch to the city's architecture. Frankfurt's Christmas markets, known as Weihnachtsmärkte, are a major highlight during this season. The Römerberg market, in particular, offers a festive atmosphere with its charming stalls selling traditional crafts, food, and mulled wine.

It's worth noting that Frankfurt is a major business and financial hub, hosting various trade fairs and conferences throughout the year. If you plan to visit for business purposes, it's advisable to check the event calendar to avoid clashes with large-scale conventions that may impact hotel availability and prices.

Ultimately, the best time to visit Frankfurt depends on your personal preferences. Whether you prefer pleasant spring weather, vibrant summer festivities, picturesque autumn landscapes, or the enchantment of winter markets, Frankfurt has something to offer year-round.

Busiest Time To Visit

The best time to visit Frankfurt, the financial and cultural center of Germany, will mainly rely on your itinerary and personal tastes. However, there are times of the year when the city enjoys a big inflow of visitors, which results in larger crowds and greater costs.

Summertime, especially in July and August, is one of the busiest periods to visit Frankfurt. This is mostly because of the ideal weather, which has comfortable temperatures and more daylight. The Main River promenade and different parks and gardens are popular outdoor attractions that many people visit during this time. It's crucial to keep in mind that during this time, hotels, eateries, and major tourist attractions frequently see significant levels of crowding and increased expenses.

The time around important trade shows and events is another hectic time in Frankfurt. The renowned exposition venue in the city, Frankfurt Messe, often holds international trade shows that draw attendees from all over the world to the city. Events like the Frankfurt Book Fair, Automechanika, and the Ambiente Fair bring sizable audiences, which boosts hotel occupancy rates and boosts activity in the city. When planning a trip during these seasons, it's best to reserve lodging well in advance to ensure availability and maybe discover lower prices.

During the holidays, especially around Christmas, Frankfurt sees an upsurge in visitor traffic. The city's holiday markets, including the well-known Frankfurt Christmas Market on the storied Römerberg Square, entice tourists with their lovely ambiance, traditional cuisine, and distinctive crafts. However, especially on weekends, the city may get rather congested at this time. To avoid the busiest times, think about going on a weekday or early in the morning.

Visit Frankfurt in the shoulder seasons if you'd want a more sedate and uncrowded experience. In comparison to the busiest summer months, spring (April to June) and fall (September to October) provide cooler weather and fewer visitors. You may still take advantage of the great weather, see the city's cultural attractions, and even get cheaper prices on lodging and travel during these times.

The summer, major trade fairs and events, and the Christmas season are the busiest periods to visit Frankfurt even though it draws tourists all year long. Consider scheduling your visit during the shoulder seasons when the city is less busy if you prefer a more laid-back experience.

Best Time To Visit in the Summer

The best time to visit Frankfurt in the summer is typically between June and August. During this period, the city experiences warm and pleasant weather,

25

making it ideal for outdoor activities and exploration.

June marks the beginning of summer in Frankfurt, and the weather starts to become warmer with temperatures ranging from 17°C to 24°C (63°F to 75°F). The city is adorned with colorful blooms, and parks and gardens are in full bloom, creating a vibrant and picturesque atmosphere. It is a great time to visit attractions like Palmengarten, a beautiful botanical garden, or take a stroll along the scenic Main River.

In July, the temperatures continue to rise, reaching highs of around 26°C to 29°C (79°F to 84°F). The days are long, providing ample daylight hours to explore the city's numerous landmarks. Take a walk through the historic Altstadt (Old Town), visit the iconic Römerberg Square, or discover the modern skyline from the Main Tower observation deck. The summer also brings various festivals and events, such as the Museumsuferfest, a cultural extravaganza celebrated along the banks of the Main River.

August in Frankfurt tends to be warm with temperatures ranging from 24°C to 28°C (75°F to 82°F). It is a perfect time to enjoy outdoor activities like picnics in the parks, bike rides along the riverbanks, or even take a day trip to the nearby Taunus Mountains for hiking. The evenings are pleasantly mild, allowing visitors to savor outdoor dining experiences or attend open-air concerts and performances.

It is worth noting that Frankfurt is a popular tourist destination, and summer attracts a significant number of visitors. Therefore, it is advisable to book accommodations and tickets to attractions in advance to ensure a smooth and enjoyable trip.

Visiting Frankfurt during the summer offers the opportunity to experience the city's vibrant atmosphere, explore its cultural heritage, and enjoy the beautiful outdoor spaces. Whether you are interested in history, or art, or simply want to soak up the summer sun, Frankfurt has something to offer during this time of the year.

Best Time To Visit in Spring

The spring season is a wonderful time to visit Frankfurt as the city comes alive with vibrant colors and pleasant weather. Spanning from March to May, the spring in Frankfurt offers a delightful mix of blooming flowers, mild temperatures, and a variety of events and festivals.

One of the best times to visit Frankfurt in the spring is during April. This month marks the beginning of spring and brings with it a sense of renewal and vitality. The city's parks and gardens, such as the Palmengarten and the Nizza Park, burst into bloom with colorful flowers and blossoming trees, creating a picturesque setting for visitors to enjoy.

Moreover, April hosts one of Frankfurt's most famous events, the Dippemess fair. This traditional folk festival takes place at the Ratsweg fairground and offers a wide range of thrilling rides, delicious food, and exciting games. It is a perfect opportunity to experience local culture and indulge in the lively atmosphere.

May is another excellent time to visit Frankfurt in the spring. The weather becomes progressively warmer, with average temperatures ranging from 12 to 20 degrees Celsius (54 to 68 degrees Fahrenheit). The longer daylight hours provide ample time to explore the city's numerous attractions, such as the historic Römerberg square, the iconic Main Tower, and the impressive St. Bartholomew's Cathedral.

In addition to pleasant weather and cultural sights, May brings forth various outdoor festivals and events in Frankfurt. The Museum Embankment Festival, held in late May, is a significant highlight. This multi-day event celebrates art, music, and culture, with museums along the embankment hosting special exhibitions, concerts, and performances. Visitors can also enjoy food stalls, live music, and a colorful fireworks display.

It's worth noting that while the spring season generally offers favorable weather conditions, it is advisable to pack layers of clothing to be prepared for occasional temperature fluctuations. It's also a good idea to check the specific dates of events and festivals in advance to plan your visit accordingly.

Visiting Frankfurt in the spring allows you to witness the city's beauty as it awakens from winter's slumber. With blooming flowers, mild temperatures, and a variety of events and festivals, April and May offer the best time to explore this bustling metropolis, immerse yourself in its rich culture, and enjoy the wonders of spring in Frankfurt.

Where to Stay in Frankfurt

There are a variety of lodging options to select from in Frankfurt, Germany, to suit different tastes and price ranges. Your unique requirements and interests will ultimately determine the perfect spot for you to stay in Frankfurt. The locations, facilities, and general attractiveness of a select few places, however, make them often suggested destinations for tourists.

The city core, often referred to as the "Innenstadt," is a well-liked spot to take into account. Numerous hotels, from opulent businesses to more moderate choices, are located in this busy neighborhood. You can reach several of Frankfurt's main sites on foot if you stay in the city center, including the famed retail strip Zeil, St. Bartholomew's Cathedral, and the historic Römerberg plaza. It is also simple to visit other areas of the city thanks to the good public transit links in the city center.

The Westend district is an additional area to take into account. In contrast to the city center, Westend provides a calmer and more residential ambiance thanks to its fine residential structures and grassy avenues. Luxury hotels, boutique hotels, and serviced flats are all mixed in this area. Public transit is readily available, and the Palmengarten, a stunning botanical park, and Goethestrasse, a renowned retail street, are both accessible on foot from the neighborhood.

For those seeking a more vibrant and trendy atmosphere, the Sachsenhausen district may be a great choice. Sachsenhausen, a city on the Main River's southern bank, is renowned for its vibrant nightlife, authentic apple wine taverns, and picturesque lanes lined with half-timbered homes. Boutique hotels and comfortable guesthouses are among the lodging options available in this region. The city center is also easily accessible on foot, or you may enjoy a lovely stroll along the river promenade.

Think about lodging in the Höchst neighborhood if you're seeking a green and tranquil setting. Höchst, is a neighborhood in the western section of Frankfurt, with a charming old town, views of the lake, and easy access to the outdoors. This region has a wide selection of hotels and guesthouses, and public transit connects it to the city center easily.

The ideal hotel in Frankfurt will ultimately rely on your interests and the reason for your trip. Frankfurt has plenty to offer for everyone, whether you like a central location, a quiet neighborhood, a bustling ambiance, or a more laid-back setting.

What to Do and See in Frankfurt

Frankfurt offers a plethora of attractions, activities, and cultural experiences for visitors. Whether you're a history buff, a food lover, an art enthusiast, or simply looking to explore a vibrant city, Frankfurt has something for everyone. Here are some recommendations on what to do and see in Frankfurt:

1. Explore the Altstadt: Start your journey in the charming Altstadt (Old Town) of Frankfurt. Marvel at the beautifully restored half-timbered houses, visit the historical Römerberg square and explore the stunning Frankfurt Cathedral (Kaiserdom).

2. Visit the Museumsufer: **Known** as the "Museum Embankment," this area is home to several world-class museums. Don't miss the Städel Museum, housing an impressive collection of European art, or the Museum of Modern Art (MMK), showcasing contemporary works. You can also explore the Museum of Communication, the German Film Museum, and many others.

3. Take a stroll in Palmengarten: **Escape** the urban hustle and immerse yourself in the serene beauty of Palmengarten. This botanical garden boasts a vast collection of exotic plants, meticulously designed landscapes, and stunning greenhouses. It's the perfect place to relax and rejuvenate.

4. Visit the Frankfurt Goethe House: **Pay homage to Germany's literary giant, Johann Wolfgang von Goethe, by visiting his birthplace. The Goethe House is now a museum dedicated to the writer's life and works, providing insights into 18th-century Frankfurt society.**

5. Explore the vibrant Zeil shopping district: **Shopaholics will find their paradise on Zeil, Frankfurt's main shopping street. Here, you can browse through an array of high-end boutiques, department stores, and local shops. Don't forget to check out the renowned MyZeil shopping center with its futuristic architecture.**

6. Admire the Main Tower: **Take an elevator ride up the Main Tower, Frankfurt's iconic**

skyscraper, for panoramic views of the city. Enjoy a breathtaking vista of the Frankfurt skyline and the meandering River Main.

7. Indulge in local cuisine: **Frankfurt is famous for its culinary delights. Don't miss the opportunity to try traditional dishes like Grüne Soße (green sauce), Handkäse mit Musik (marinated cheese), or the iconic Frankfurter Würstchen (Frankfurt sausage). Pair your meal with a glass of Apfelwein (apple wine) for an authentic experience.**

8. Attend a trade fair or event: **Frankfurt is a major hub for trade fairs and exhibitions. Check the event calendar to see if any interesting events align with your visit. Events like the Frankfurt Book Fair or the Christmas Market are particularly popular.**

These are just a few highlights of what Frankfurt has to offer. The city's rich history, cultural diversity, and modern charm make it an exciting destination for travelers. Whether you're interested in architecture, arts, cuisine, or simply soaking up the vibrant atmosphere, Frankfurt will surely captivate you.

What to Bring to Frankfurt

When packing for your trip to Frankfurt, it's essential to consider the city's climate, attractions, and personal needs. Frankfurt, located in Germany, experiences a temperate seasonal climate with mild summers and chilly winters. Here's a list of items you should consider bringing to

Frankfurt to ensure a comfortable and enjoyable stay.

1. Clothing: Pack clothing suitable for the weather conditions during your visit. In summer (June to August), bring lightweight and breathable clothes such as T-shirts, shorts, and dresses. Don't forget a light jacket or sweater for cooler evenings. In winter (December to February), pack warm clothes, including sweaters, coats, hats, gloves, and scarves, as temperatures can drop below freezing.

2. Comfortable Shoes: Frankfurt is a city known for its walking culture, with many attractions located close to each other. Bring comfortable walking shoes or sneakers to explore the city's vibrant streets, museums, and parks.

3. Travel Adaptors: **Germany uses the Europlug (Type C) and Schuko plug (Type F) for electrical outlets. Depending on your home country, you may need a travel adaptor to charge your electronic devices. It's always a good idea to carry a universal travel adaptor to ensure compatibility.**

4. Travel Documents: **Don't forget to bring your passport, visa (if required), and any other necessary travel documents. It's also recommended to make copies of these documents and keep them separately in case of loss or theft.**

5. Medications: **If you take prescription medications, ensure you have an adequate supply for the duration of your stay. It's also wise to carry a small first aid kit containing essentials like band-aids, pain relievers, and any personal medications you might need.**

6. Currency: **It's advisable to have some cash in Euros for small expenses like public transportation, cafes, and shops that might not accept cards. You can also use credit or debit cards, but it's essential to inform your bank of your travel plans to avoid any issues.**

7. Travel Insurance: **Consider purchasing travel insurance to protect yourself against unforeseen circumstances like trip cancellations, medical emergencies, or lost luggage. Check the coverage details and make sure it aligns with your needs.**

8. Guidebook or Map: **A guidebook or a map of Frankfurt can help navigate the city and discover its landmarks, attractions, and local recommendations. Alternatively, you can use digital maps or travel apps on your smartphone.**

9. Weather Essentials: Depending on the season, pack weather-specific items such as sunscreen, sunglasses, and a hat for summer, or an umbrella and waterproof jacket for rainy periods.

10. Language Resources: While many people in Frankfurt speak English, it's always useful to carry a pocket phrasebook or have a translation app on your phone to assist with basic communication or understanding local signage.

Remember to pack efficiently and consider the duration of your trip when deciding how much to bring. Frankfurt offers a mix of history, culture, and modern attractions, so make sure you have everything you need to fully enjoy your visit to this dynamic German city.

CHAPTER 2: GETTING AROUND IN FRANKFURT

ICE 3 High Speed Train at Frankfurt Long-Distance Station. Germany

Frankfurt's Public Transportation

Frankfurt is famous for having a robust and effective public transit system. Residents and tourists may easily get about the city and its environs thanks to a well-connected network of trains, trams, buses, and underground lines. Frankfurt's public transit system provides ease, dependability, and sustainability, making it the method of transportation of choice for many.

The regional rail system run by Deutsche Bahn (DB) serves as the foundation of Frankfurt's public transportation system. Frankfurt Hauptbahnhof, the city's top-notch mainline station, is a key hub for transportation linking different parts of Germany and its neighbors. From here, commuters may easily travel inside Frankfurt and beyond thanks to access to both local and long-distance trains.

Frankfurt has a sizable tram and bus network in addition to the regional rail network. With accessible links to several areas and important landmarks, the tram system completely encompasses the city. Passengers can depend on trams to get them to their destinations on time since they operate often and are renowned for being prompt. Similarly, by reaching places that trams do not serve, the bus network completes the tram system. Modern amenities on the buses, including wheelchair accessibility and real-time passenger information systems, improve the entire travel experience.

A well-designed underground (U-Bahn) system, with many lines that serve both the city center and the suburbs, is another asset of Frankfurt. Particularly during rush hour when traffic is heavy, the U-Bahn provides a fast and effective form of transit. The trains operate at regular intervals, giving locals and visitors a dependable way to commute.

The integration of many means of transportation under a single ticketing system is one of Frankfurt's public transportation system's distinguishing characteristics. The Rhein-Main Verkehrsverbund (RMV), a regional transportation organization, is in charge of managing rates and tickets for different public transportation options. Passengers can move easily between trains, trams, buses, and the U-Bahn by using a single ticket for several trips. This comprehensive strategy makes travel easier and promotes the use of public transit as a practical substitute for private automobiles.

Frankfurt is also devoted to sustainability and has launched several programs to encourage environmentally friendly mobility. With a vast network of bike lanes and designated parking spaces, the city promotes the use of bicycles. Additionally, the introduction of electric buses in recent years has decreased both noise pollution and carbon emissions.

Frankfurt's public transportation network is a well-established, dependable, and environmentally friendly one that effectively links the city and its surrounding areas. Residents and tourists can easily explore the city and take advantage of the advantages of quick and environmentally friendly transit thanks to its comprehensive network of trains, trams, buses, and the U-Bahn. The integration of several transportation options via a single ticketing system significantly improves the quality of the journey. Frankfurt's dedication to public transit demonstrates how cutting-edge it is and how important efficient mobility is to its citizens.

Car Rental

If you're planning a trip to Frankfurt, Germany, and looking for convenient and flexible transportation options, car rentals can be an excellent choice. Frankfurt is a bustling city with a rich history, vibrant culture, and numerous attractions to explore. Renting a car gives you the freedom to navigate the city and its surroundings at your own pace, allowing you to make the most of your visit.

Frankfurt offers a wide range of car rental services catering to different budgets and preferences. You can find several reputable international car rental companies, such as Avis, Hertz, Europcar, and Sixt, as well as local providers. These companies have branches located at Frankfurt Airport, major train stations, and in the city center, making it convenient to pick up and drop off your rental vehicle.

When renting a car in Frankfurt, it's essential to consider a few factors. Firstly, make sure you have a valid driver's license and meet the age requirements set by the rental company, which is typically 21 years old or older. Additionally, most rental companies require a credit card for the reservation and deposit. It's advisable to book your car in advance, especially during peak travel seasons, to ensure availability and secure better rates.

Frankfurt's central location in Germany makes it an ideal starting point for exploring the surrounding areas. With a rental car, you can easily venture beyond the city limits and visit nearby destinations like the picturesque Rhine Valley, the historic town of Heidelberg, or the charming villages of the Taunus Mountains. Having a car also allows you to take day trips to cities like Cologne, Stuttgart, or Nuremberg, which are within a few hours' drive.

While driving in Frankfurt, it's crucial to familiarize yourself with the local traffic rules and regulations. In Germany, vehicles drive on the right side of the road, and speed limits are strictly enforced. Frankfurt has an extensive network of well-maintained roads, and highways connect the city to other major cities and regions in Germany. However, it's worth noting that parking in the city center can be challenging and expensive, so it's advisable to use public parking facilities or opt for accommodations that provide parking spaces.

Renting a car in Frankfurt can enhance your travel experience, allowing you to explore the city and its surroundings with convenience and flexibility. By choosing a reputable rental company and following the necessary guidelines, you can embark on an unforgettable journey through this vibrant part of Germany. Enjoy your trip and happy driving!

Buses

The efficient and dependable public transit system in Frankfurt, Germany, is greatly dependent on bus service. Buses are a popular alternative for locals and tourists alike due to their broad coverage, contemporary fleet, and practical scheduling.

The Rhein-Main-Verkehrsverbund (RMV), which runs Frankfurt's bus system, maintains smooth communication with other public transportation options including trams, trains, and the U-Bahn (subway). Bus travel is a practical choice for moving about the city because of this integration, which makes it simple for passengers to switch between various means of transportation.

The vast coverage of bus transit in Frankfurt is one of its main benefits. Buses provide transportation to practically all of the city's neighborhoods and economic sectors, as well as to popular tourist destinations. No matter where they live or work, citizens will always have access to public transit thanks to this extensive network. The bus system serves as a handy means for visitors to experience the city's sites and attractions.

The buses themselves are up-to-date and well-maintained, with plush seats, ac, and other amenities to improve the traveling experience. Additionally, many buses include ramps or low floors to make boarding simpler for passengers with impairments, strollers, or bulky baggage.

Frankfurt has dependable and consistent bus timetables, with buses arriving at regular intervals throughout the day. By knowing that they won't have to wait too long for the next bus, travelers can properly plan their routes. The timetables are coordinated with other public transportation systems to provide for seamless transfers and short wait times.

To meet varied demands, Frankfurt's bus system also provides a variety of ticket choices. Depending on their travel needs, passengers may choose between single-ride tickets, day passes, weekly passes, or monthly passes. Additionally, the RMV provides integrated ticketing, enabling users to travel on the RMV network with a single ticket on several occasions and for various means of transportation.

Frankfurt's public transportation system is not complete without the use of buses. Buses provide a dependable and effective way to move about the city because of their wide coverage, current fleet, flexible scheduling, and integration with other forms of transportation. Whether you're a local traveling to work or a visitor taking in the sights, Frankfurt's bus system provides a practical and easy method to get about.

Travel Tips

Frankfurtis a city that seamlessly blends modernity with historical charm. If you're planning a visit to this bustling metropolis, here are some travel tips to help you make the most of your trip:

1. Weather and Season: **Frankfurt** experiences a temperate climate, with mild winters and warm summers. Pack accordingly, and check the weather forecast before your trip to ensure you have appropriate clothing for the season. Remember to carry an umbrella or raincoat, as rain showers can occur throughout the year.

2. Public Transportation: **Frankfurt** boasts an efficient and well-connected public transportation system. The city's extensive network of trains, trams, and buses makes it

easy to navigate and explore. Consider purchasing a Frankfurt Card, which offers unlimited travel on public transportation and discounted entry to many attractions.

3. Language: German is the official language in Frankfurt, but many locals also speak English, especially in tourist areas. It's helpful to learn a few basic German phrases, such as greetings and polite expressions, to enhance your interactions with the locals.

4. Currency: The currency used in Frankfurt, and throughout Germany, is the Euro (€). It's advisable to carry some cash for smaller establishments that may not accept cards. ATMs are widely available, and credit cards are generally accepted in most places.

5. Must-See Attractions: Frankfurt offers a rich tapestry of cultural and historical

attractions. Don't miss the iconic Römerberg, the historic square with charming half-timbered houses, and visit the impressive Frankfurt Cathedral. Explore the art collections at the Städel Museum or take a stroll along the picturesque Main River.

6. Cuisine: Indulge in Frankfurt's culinary delights by trying local specialties such as "Frankfurter Grüne Sauce" (a tangy herb sauce) and "Apfelwein" (a traditional apple cider). Don't forget to visit Kleinmarkthalle, a bustling indoor market offering a wide range of fresh produce, delicacies, and street food.

7. Safety: Frankfurt is generally a safe city, but it's always wise to take precautions. Keep an eye on your belongings, especially in crowded tourist areas, and be cautious of

pickpockets. It's advisable to carry a photocopy of your passport and important documents while keeping the originals in a safe place.

8. Day Trips: Take advantage of Frankfurt's central location to explore nearby attractions. Visit the charming town of Heidelberg with its famous castle or venture into the scenic Rhine Valley, known for its picturesque vineyards and medieval castles.

By keeping these travel tips in mind, you'll be well-prepared to enjoy your time in Frankfurt. Embrace the city's unique blend of history, culture, and modernity, and create lasting memories in this captivating destination.

CHAPTER 3: EXPLORING FRANKFURT

Park bench with view on Frankfurt am Main

National Parks and Preserves

Frankfurt is a bustling city filled with skyscrapers, commerce, and a vibrant urban lifestyle. However, amidst the hustle and bustle, Frankfurt also offers several natural escapes in the form of national parks and preserves. These protected areas provide a breath of fresh air and a chance to immerse oneself in nature, away from the urban environment. Let's explore some of the notable national parks and preserves in Frankfurt.

The Taunus Nature Park, located just a short drive away from Frankfurt, is a vast expanse of rolling hills, dense forests, and picturesque landscapes. Covering an area of approximately 1,500 square kilometers, it offers a range of outdoor activities such as hiking, cycling, and wildlife spotting. The park is home to diverse flora and fauna, including deer, wild boar, and various bird species. The Feldberg, the highest peak in the Taunus range, offers panoramic views of the surrounding countryside and is a popular destination for nature enthusiasts.

Another notable natural area near Frankfurt is the Odenwald Nature Park. Situated on the eastern slopes of the Rhine Valley, this park is characterized by its dense forests, tranquil rivers, and charming villages. Hiking trails crisscross the landscape, allowing visitors to explore the picturesque scenery and discover hidden gems such as ancient ruins and castles. The park is also known for its diverse wildlife, including eagles, lynx, and otters.

For those interested in river ecosystems, the Rhine-Main Reserve is a must-visit. This nature reserve, located along the banks of the River Rhine, is a haven for waterfowl and other wetland species. It provides vital habitats for migratory birds, and birdwatchers can spot a wide variety of species throughout the year. The reserve also offers opportunities for boating, fishing, and picnicking along the riverbanks.

In addition to these natural areas, Frankfurt itself boasts several urban parks and green spaces that offer a refreshing retreat within the city. The Palmengarten, for instance, is a botanical garden that features a vast collection of plants from around the world. It offers a tranquil oasis where visitors can stroll through themed gardens, relax by the pond, or enjoy a picnic on the lawns.

Frankfurt and its surrounding regions offer a wealth of natural wonders in the form of national parks, nature reserves, and urban green spaces. These areas provide a welcome respite from city life, allowing visitors to connect with nature, engage in outdoor activities, and appreciate the beauty of the natural world. Whether it's exploring the Taunus hills, wandering through the Odenwald forests, or enjoying the tranquility of the Rhine-Main Reserve, Frankfurt has something to offer for every nature lover.

Outdoor Activities

Frankfurt is home to a lively metropolitan environment in addition to a wide range of outdoor pursuits for adventurers and nature lovers. Frankfurt welcomes citizens and tourists alike to walk outdoors and enjoy the beauty of its natural surroundings with its stunning parks and gardens as well as tranquil riverbank promenades. In this article, we'll discuss some of the amazing outdoor activities you may enjoy in this energetic city.

1. Take a stroll around Palmengarten: Palmengarten, a 50-acre botanical wonderland near Frankfurt, is a gorgeous collection of plants from all over the globe. This lush sanctuary is ideal for leisurely strolls, picnics, or just resting among nature's beauty with its perfectly maintained landscapes, vibrant flower beds, and peaceful ponds.

2. Explore the Main River: The Main River is a key component of Frankfurt's appeal and provides a wealth of outdoor recreation choices. Rent a bike and enjoy a leisurely ride along the lovely shoreline, or go on a scenic boat trip along the river. The lovely cafés and beer gardens that line the

riverbanks provide the ideal place to relax and take in the lively energy of the city.

3. Go to the Frankfurt City Forest: **This huge forest retreat is immediately outside the city, a great place to get away from the hustle and bustle of the metropolis. This verdant forest encourages hikers, runners, and bikers to explore its varied flora and wildlife thanks to its large network of routes. Take a stop at one of the secluded picnic spots or climb the Goetheturm tower for sweeping views of the surroundings.**

4. Take in the Grüneburgpark: **Located in the center of Frankfurt, the Grüneburgpark provides a peaceful escape from the bustle of the city. Explore its well-kept lawns, fragrant rose gardens, and lovely water features on a leisurely walk. The Palm House, a stunning glass conservatory where**

visitors may immerse themselves in a tropical paradise, is another feature of the park.

5. Set out on the Lohrberg Vineyard Trail: The Lohrberg Vineyard Trail is a must-visit location for wine connoisseurs and nature lovers. You may enjoy breath-taking views of the Frankfurt skyline and the surrounding countryside as you stroll along this picturesque walk through the city's lovely vineyards. Take in the tranquility of the magnificent views or partake in a wine-tasting session at one of the nearby wineries.

There is something for everyone to enjoy thanks to the variety of interests that Frankfurt's outdoor activities cater to. Frankfurt's natural attractions provide a pleasant respite from the metropolitan environment, whether you like tranquil gardens, lovely river walks, or energizing excursions through lush woods. Therefore, take a break from the city's busy streets and immerse yourself in Frankfurt's invigorating outdoor delights.

Nature Tour

Frankfurt is not only known for its finance and business hub but also for its stunning natural landscapes and picturesque surroundings. A nature tour in Frankfurt offers visitors a refreshing escape from the urban chaos and provides an opportunity to immerse themselves in the beauty of the outdoors.

70

One of the must-visit destinations for nature enthusiasts is the Frankfurt City Forest, also known as the Stadtwald. Spanning over 48 square kilometers, this vast woodland is a green oasis located just a few minutes away from the city center. It boasts an extensive network of trails that wind through lush forests, meadows, and tranquil lakes. Exploring the City Forest on foot or by bicycle allows visitors to enjoy the peaceful ambiance, observe various wildlife species, and breathe in the fresh air.

For those seeking a more picturesque experience, a visit to the Palmengarten is highly recommended. This exquisite botanical garden showcases an impressive array of plant species from around the world. Spanning 22 hectares, the

Palmengarten features beautifully landscaped gardens, themed sections, and several greenhouses. Visitors can take strolls through the colorful flower beds, relax in serene ponds, or simply find a quiet spot to read a book amidst nature's tranquility.

Nature lovers should also make a stop at the Main River, which flows through the heart of Frankfurt. The riverbank offers scenic views, especially during sunset when the city's skyline is bathed in a golden glow. Walking or cycling along the river promenade is a popular activity, providing an opportunity to enjoy the river breeze, watch boats sail by, and witness the vibrant atmosphere of the city.

Another gem of natural beauty near Frankfurt is the Taunus Mountains. Located just a short distance from the city, this mountain range is a haven for hikers and outdoor enthusiasts. The Taunus offers a diverse range of trails, from leisurely walks to challenging hikes, catering to all fitness levels. As you ascend the peaks, you'll be rewarded with breathtaking vistas of rolling hills, dense forests, and picturesque valleys.

A nature tour in Frankfurt unveils a different side of this bustling city, showcasing its natural wonders and inviting visitors to relax, unwind, and reconnect with the outdoors. Whether it's exploring the City Forest, wandering through the Palmengarten, enjoying the Main River's serenity, or venturing into the Taunus

Mountains, nature lovers will find plenty to appreciate in Frankfurt's green spaces. So, take a break from the urban chaos and embark on a nature tour in Frankfurt to rejuvenate your mind, body, and soul amidst the beauty of Mother Nature.

CHAPTER 4: SHOPPING AND NIGHTLIFE

Food and Drink

Frankfurt is well-known for its wide and delightful food and drink scene in addition to its financial prowess. Frankfurt provides a variety of gastronomic pleasures to suit all interests and inclinations, whether you're a native or a guest.

Without discussing the Frankfurt sausage, sometimes referred to as "Frankfurter," one cannot

explain Frankfurt's culinary scene. These thin, juicy pig sausages are often served with sauerkraut and mustard and are sometimes  eaten in a bread roll known as a "Brötchen." These delectable sausages are available in nearby delis, eateries, and even the renowned outdoor market, Kleinmarkthalle. To complete the experience, don't forget to enjoy them with a glass of apple wine, which is unique to the area.

Speaking of apple wine, Frankfurters have a soft spot in their hearts for this delightful libation. Apple wine, or "Apfelwein," is a somewhat sour and fizzy beverage made from locally produced apples that are relished both chilled and in its stronger version, known as "Ebbelwoi." It's a popular beverage that fosters community, and the city is full of "Ebbelwoi-Lokale," or traditional apple wine pubs. These homey places provide a pleasant setting for enjoying the flavor of this local delicacy.

Frankfurt won't let down those looking for a larger variety of foreign tastes. The city is a cultural melting pot, creating a thriving food scene with a wide range of alternatives. Frankfurt offers everything from authentic German restaurants to Italian trattorias, Asian fusion restaurants, and Middle Eastern cafes. The various restaurants and pubs in Sachsenhausen, a district noted for its vibrant nightlife, are especially well-known for serving food from all over the globe.

Frankfurt's food markets also demonstrate its dedication to excellence and sustainability. With its extensive selection of fresh vegetables, cheeses, meats, baked products, and exotic delicacies, the aforementioned Kleinmarkthalle is a foodie's delight. It's the ideal location to learn about the regional cuisine and to buy supplies for a picnic in one of Frankfurt's beautiful parks.

Frankfurt also holds several food-related festivals and events all year long to celebrate cuisine and regional specialties. Indulge in local dishes while enjoying live music and entertainment at the Mainfest, a summer event held along the banks of the River Main.

Frankfurt provides a gastronomic experience that appeals to all tastes. This dynamic city offers a wide variety of food and drinks alternatives to satiate your needs, whether you like traditional German cooking or are in the mood for exotic tastes.

Come and immerse yourself in Frankfurt's culinary scene to experience the mouth watering delicacies this city has to offer.

Traditional Dishes

Frankfurt is not only known for its towering skyscrapers and financial district but also for its rich culinary heritage. The traditional dishes of Frankfurt reflect the region's history, culture, and local ingredients, making them a delight for food enthusiasts.

One iconic dish that Frankfurt is famous for is "Frankfurter Grüne Soße" or Frankfurt Green Sauce. It consists of a mixture of seven fresh herbs, including parsley, chives, sorrel, borage, cress, burnet, and salad burnet, blended with sour cream and yogurt. This tangy and refreshing sauce is often served with boiled potatoes and either hard-boiled eggs or a succulent piece of locally sourced meat.

Another beloved dish is "Frankfurter Rippchen." These are succulent and tender pork chops that are brined and then boiled in a flavorful broth until they are juicy and fall-off-the-bone tender. They are traditionally served with sauerkraut, mashed potatoes, and a dollop of mustard.

If you're a fan of sausages, you cannot miss trying the famous "Frankfurter Würstchen." These are small, lightly smoked pork sausages made with finely ground meat and a blend of spices. They are typically served with sauerkraut or potato salad and enjoyed with a side of mustard.

For those seeking a hearty and filling dish, "Handkäse mit Musik" is a must-try. It consists of a tangy and pungent cheese called Handkäse marinated in a dressing made of onions, vinegar, oil, and spices. It is often accompanied by a slice of rye bread and enjoyed as a snack or appetizer.

Lastly, "Bethmännchen" is a delightful traditional dessert originating from Frankfurt. These small marzipan cookies are made with ground almonds, powdered sugar, rosewater, and topped with three almond halves to represent the four sons of the famous Frankfurt banker Simon Moritz von Bethmann. They are a popular treat during the Christmas season.

Frankfurt's traditional dishes offer a diverse range of flavors, from tangy and refreshing to rich and savory. They provide a glimpse into the culinary traditions and local ingredients that have shaped the region's gastronomy. Whether you're a visitor or a local, exploring these dishes is a delightful way to immerse yourself in Frankfurt's vibrant food culture.

Eating Out

Frankfurt provides a fantastic dining experience that combines traditional German cuisine with delicacies from across the world. Frankfurt is recognized for its great food scene and offers a broad variety of alternatives to suit all tastes and budgets. Frankfurt is a bustling and varied city.

Enjoying genuine German cuisine is one of the best parts of dining out in Frankfurt. Traditional German food is readily accessible in a variety of restaurants and beer gardens across the city, from substantial sausages and schnitzels to delectable pretzels and sauerkraut. Visitors may savor local dishes including Frankfurter Rippchen (smoked pork chops), Handkäse mit Musik (a strong cheese dish), and Grüne Soße (a tart herb sauce).

International cuisines are also a melting pot in Frankfurt. The city's multiracial population has helped to create a culinary scene that is diversified, with restaurants serving cuisine from all over the world. You may locate a restaurant that will satiate your appetite for Italian spaghetti, Lebanese kebabs, Indian curries, or Japanese sushi.

The city's historic Apfelwein (apple wine) pubs and quaint cider taverns are famous for being located in the Alt-Sachsenhausen neighborhood and city center, respectively. With substantial delicacies like Handkäs mit Musik or Frankfurt-style sausages, you can relax here in a rustic setting while drinking the regional specialty.

Frankfurt has several Michelin-starred restaurants that provide upscale fare for customers looking for a special dining experience. To provide a remarkable dining experience, these businesses bring together excellent tastes, attractive displays, and outstanding service.

Frankfurt is well-known for its vibrant food markets in addition to its extensive selection of eateries. Foodies often visit the Kleinmarkthalle, which has a lively ambiance and a wide selection of fresh foods including meats, cheeses, and fruits. It's the ideal location to learn about and taste regional foods while absorbing the lively market atmosphere.

And lastly, Frankfurt celebrates a variety of culinary themes throughout the year with several food festivals and events. For instance, the annual Museumsuferfest offers a variety of different cuisines across the Main River, together with live entertainment and cultural displays.

Dining out in Frankfurt is a fascinating experience that mixes customary German fare with cuisines from across the world and a buzzing dining scene. The city has something to satisfy every appetite and inclination, from historic pubs to Michelin-starred restaurants and lively food markets. Anyone visiting Frankfurt who wants to experience regional tastes and indulge in a wide variety of gastronomic pleasures must explore the city's culinary offers.

CHAPTER 5: WHAT TO DO BEFORE TRAVELING

Entry Requirements

Travelers on business, vacations, and expatriates love to visit Frankfurt, a vivacious and multicultural city in the center of Germany. To guarantee a hassle-free trip, it's crucial to acquaint yourself with the admission criteria if you're thinking of visiting Frankfurt.

The majority of visitors' nationality, the reason for their trip, and the length of their stay all affect Frankfurt's admission criteria. You only need to have a current passport or national identification card to visit Frankfurt if you are a citizen of one of the European Union (EU) or European

Economic Area (EEA) member states. The residents of Switzerland, Iceland, Liechtenstein, and Norway are also subject to this. A visa or any other kind of supporting document is not required.

Entry criteria for residents of nations outside the EU/EEA may differ. Numerous nations and Germany have an agreement that exempts its residents from needing visas for stays of up to 90 days for either business or vacation. Before departing for Frankfurt, it is important to confirm the precise visa requirements for your country of citizenship. The website of the German embassy or consulate in your country is the greatest source for precise and current information.

You should probably apply for a visa in advance of your trip if you want to remain in Frankfurt for some time longer than 90 days or if you have another reason for visiting, such as to work, study, or be with family. The kind of visa you need depends depend on the purpose of your trip, so start the application procedure well in advance to give yourself enough time for processing.

It's important to keep in mind that the German authorities may still ask for extra supporting papers, such as evidence of lodging, travel insurance, financial means, and a return ticket, even if you meet the criteria for a visa. The immigration procedure will go more smoothly and quickly if you have these papers on hand when you enter Frankfurt.

In addition, normal entrance criteria apply to all visitors, regardless of country, including holding a passport that is valid and has at least six months left on its validity from the date of admission. Furthermore, it's crucial to adhere to customs laws governing the import and export of commodities, including currency restrictions.

The admission criteria for Frankfurt vary according to the visitor's country, intended use for the trip, and planned length of stay. The only entry requirements for certain nationals are a valid passport or national identification card, while others may need a visa. To guarantee a smooth entrance into Frankfurt and a pleasant stay in the city, it is essential to learn about and adhere to the particular rules relevant to your circumstances.

Travel Restrictions

As of my knowledge cutoff in September 2021, I can provide you with general information about travel restrictions in Frankfurt. However, please note that the situation might have changed since then, and it's essential to refer to up-to-date sources such as official government websites or travel advisories for the most accurate and current information.

Frankfurt, as a major city in Germany, is subject to travel restrictions that are implemented by the German government and may be influenced by regional or global circumstances. These restrictions are put in place to manage and control the spread of infectious diseases, such as the COVID-19 pandemic.

Travel restrictions can include various measures, such as entry requirements, quarantine regulations, and testing protocols. The specific rules and guidelines can change over time based on the prevailing health situation.

When planning a trip to Frankfurt, it's important to consider the entry requirements for Germany as a whole. As of my knowledge cutoff, travelers from certain countries may be required to obtain a visa or travel authorization before entering Germany. Additionally, travelers may need to provide a negative COVID-19 test result, undergo health screenings, or complete a quarantine period upon arrival.

Furthermore, the German government has the authority to enforce regional or localized restrictions depending on the infection rates in specific areas, including Frankfurt. These measures can include lockdowns, curfews, or limitations on public gatherings.

To stay updated on the current travel restrictions in Frankfurt, it is advisable to consult official sources such as the German Federal Foreign Office, the Robert Koch Institute, or the Frankfurt Airport website. These sources provide accurate and reliable information regarding entry requirements, quarantine guidelines, and any other travel-related restrictions that may be in effect.

Given that my information is based on pre-2021 knowledge, it's crucial to verify the most recent travel guidelines and restrictions before planning any trip to Frankfurt or any other destination.

Travel Insurance

Any trip must include travel insurance, and one to Frankfurt, Germany is no exception. It draws a sizable number of visitors each year as a lively city with a rich cultural history and various attractions. Whether you're arranging a quick business trip or a relaxing vacation, having travel insurance may provide you with financial security and peace of mind in the event of unforeseen circumstances.

Frankfurt, a significant international center, provides a variety of visitor-specific travel insurance solutions. Medical crises, travel disruptions or cancellations, lost or delayed luggage, and personal responsibility are all commonly covered under these plans. Medical insurance is especially important since it makes sure you have access to high-quality medical treatment without having to pay expensive prices if you become sick or hurt while you're there.

It's crucial to take the policy's coverage limitations, exclusions, and deductibles into account while choosing travel insurance in Frankfurt. You can make a more educated choice if you read the small print and comprehend the terms and conditions. Additionally, confirm if the coverage provides round-the-clock emergency assistance, since having a solid support network may be quite helpful in unexpected situations.

Although it is not required to get travel insurance to enter Frankfurt, it is strongly advised. If you don't have enough insurance, you can end up having to pay a lot of money if anything unexpected happens. Travel insurance may cover your non-refundable costs, for instance if a sudden sickness compels you to postpone your vacation or your flight is canceled due to bad weather. The insurance might also pay for the expense of replacing necessary things if your luggage is delayed or lost.

Be sure to consider your unique requirements and the purpose of your trip before buying travel insurance. Think about things like how long you want to stay, the activities you want to do, and any current medical issues. These specifics will assist you in choosing a policy that offers the right level of protection.

Purchasing travel insurance before going to Frankfurt is a smart move. It protects you against possible threats and offers financial security while you're traveling. You may travel with confidence and take advantage of your stay in this exciting city by selecting a reputable insurance provider and carefully reading the policy terms.

What Vaccination Do I Need

Planning a trip to Frankfurt? As you prepare for your exciting adventure, it is essential to prioritize your health and safety. One of the crucial steps you can take is to ensure that you are adequately vaccinated. Vaccination plays a vital role in protecting yourself and others from preventable diseases, and it is especially important when traveling to new destinations. This note emphasizes the significance of vaccination for your Frankfurt trip and highlights key reasons why it is necessary.

1. Disease Prevention: **Vaccinations safeguard against infectious diseases that can be prevalent in different regions. By getting vaccinated before your Frankfurt trip, you reduce the risk of contracting and spreading diseases such as measles, influenza, hepatitis, and more. These diseases can be easily transmitted in crowded spaces like airports, public transportation, and tourist attractions. By taking the necessary vaccines, you contribute to maintaining a healthy environment for both yourself and the local population.**

2. Personal Safety: **Your vaccination status directly affects your safety during travel. Being immunized helps protect you from potential health hazards and minimizes the likelihood of falling seriously ill. This is**

particularly crucial if you have any underlying health conditions or if you are planning to visit Frankfurt during flu season or a period of increased disease activity. Vaccination boosts your immune system, equipping your body to fight off infections and reducing the severity of symptoms if you do get sick.

3. Travel Requirements: Some countries and destinations, including Germany, may have specific vaccination requirements for entry. Ensuring that you are up to date with the necessary vaccinations not only keeps you compliant with travel regulations but also prevents any inconvenience or denial of entry upon arrival in Frankfurt. Before your trip, research the specific vaccination recommendations or requirements for

Germany and consult with your healthcare provider to ensure compliance.

Prioritizing vaccination is a responsible step to protect your health, the health of those around you, and the communities you visit. It reduces the risk of contracting and spreading diseases, enhances personal safety, and helps you meet travel requirements. As you plan your trip to Frankfurt, consult with your healthcare provider to assess your vaccination needs and ensure that you are fully protected. Remember, a well-prepared and vaccinated traveler is an empowered traveler, ready to explore Frankfurt with confidence and peace of mind.

Familiarize Yourself with the Currency

Currencies in Frankfurt play a significant role in the financial landscape of both Germany and the European Union. As one of the major financial centers in Europe, Frankfurt is home to various currencies, with the euro being the primary currency in circulation.

The euro (€) is the official currency of Germany and is widely accepted throughout Frankfurt. Introduced in 2002, the euro replaced the Deutsche Mark as the country's national currency. As a member of the Eurozone, Germany is part of a monetary union that comprises 19 European Union member states. This means that Frankfurt benefits from the stability and convenience of a shared currency, facilitating trade and investment within the region.

Given Frankfurt's position as the financial hub of Germany, foreign currencies also have a presence in the city. Major international currencies like the US dollar (USD), British pound (GBP), Japanese yen (JPY), and Swiss franc (CHF) can be exchanged at banks, currency exchange offices, and many hotels in Frankfurt. The city's international airport and its numerous international businesses attract a diverse range of visitors and expatriates, creating a demand for foreign currencies.

Moreover, Frankfurt is home to the European Central Bank (ECB), which plays a crucial role in the management of the euro and the stability of the Eurozone. The ECB is responsible for formulating and implementing monetary policy, including setting interest rates and maintaining price stability. Its decisions influence not only the local economy but also have a broader impact on the European Union and global financial markets.

In addition to traditional currencies, Frankfurt has also been at the forefront of the digital currency revolution. As blockchain technology and cryptocurrencies gain momentum, Frankfurt has emerged as a key center for cryptocurrency exchanges and fintech innovation. Cryptocurrencies like Bitcoin, Ethereum, and others are traded and regulated in the city, further diversifying the currency landscape and attracting investors and entrepreneurs from around the world.

Frankfurt's currency ecosystem is characterized by the dominance of the euro as the official currency, supplemented by the presence of major international currencies and the growing influence of digital currencies. This diversity reflects the city's status as a financial powerhouse, facilitating international trade, investment, and financial transactions. Whether conducting business or visiting Frankfurt as a tourist, individuals can easily access a variety of currencies to suit their needs, making the city an attractive destination for both financial and leisure activities.

General Safety Tips

Frankfurt is a bustling city that draws visitors from all over the globe due to its gorgeous skyline and extensive history. Even though Frankfurt is often a safe place to visit, it's still vital to exercise care to make sure your vacation is safe and easy. Following is some general safety advice you should consider while there:

1. Take care of your possessions: Like any other well-known tourist location, Frankfurt sometimes experiences petty theft. Be careful when you go, particularly in busy places, on public transit, and at popular tourist destinations. Keep your belongings safe. To conceal your passport, money, and

cards, think about wearing a money belt or concealed bag.

2. Maintain local knowledge: **Become acquainted with Frankfurt's and Germany's general local laws and traditions. To prevent any accidental insult, respect cultural customs and act correctly. It's usually a good idea to be able to speak with locals and ask for help if necessary by knowing a few simple German words.**

3. Take a dependable mode of transportation: **Frankfurt's rail, tram, and bus networks are all effective. To safeguard your safety, use authorized taxis or reputable ride-sharing services. Refrain from getting in unmarked or unapproved cars.**

4. Be on the lookout for frauds: Tourist hotspots may serve as a fertile ground for scammers. Keep an eye out for anybody approaching you with shady offers or demands for cash, and be wary of them. Be cautious of street sellers who use distracting sales techniques or who offer fake items.

5. Select reliable lodging: Give top priority to booking stays at hotels or other lodgings with a good reputation. To guarantee a secure and enjoyable stay, research your alternatives ahead and read reviews from prior visitors. Check that your lodging has security measures like safe locks, security cameras, and emergency exits.

6. Keep in touch: While visiting Frankfurt, be sure you have a dependable method of contact. Maintain a full charge on your phone and think about getting a local SIM

card or an international data package. In case of an emergency, have emergency phone numbers handy, including those of your embassy and the local government.

7. Keep up with travel warnings: Before your journey, check the most current updates and travel advisories for Frankfurt. Keep abreast of any dangers or security issues and modify your preparations as necessary.

Keep in mind that the purpose of these safety recommendations is to improve your trip overall while reducing any possible dangers. You may take comfort in being able to safely enjoy Frankfurt's lovely city by being aware, knowledgeable, and organized.

Health Safety Consideration

When planning a trip to Frankfurt, it is important to prioritize health and safety to ensure a smooth and enjoyable experience. Here are some essential considerations to keep in mind:

1. COVID-19 Precautions: The COVID-19 pandemic remains a concern. Stay updated with the latest travel advisories and regulations from reputable sources such as the World Health Organization (WHO) and local health authorities. Follow guidelines related to vaccination requirements, testing protocols, mask mandates, and social distancing measures.

2. Travel Insurance: Obtain comprehensive travel insurance that covers medical expenses, trip cancellation or interruption, and emergency medical evacuation. It

provides peace of mind in case unforeseen circumstances arise during your trip.

3. Vaccinations and Medications: Ensure that your routine vaccinations are up to date. Consult with your healthcare provider regarding any additional vaccinations recommended for travel to Germany. Carry a sufficient supply of necessary medications, along with prescriptions, in case you require them during your trip.

4. Hygiene Practices: Maintain good hygiene habits to reduce the risk of illness. Wash your hands frequently with soap and water for at least 20 seconds, or use hand sanitizer with at least 60% alcohol content. Avoid touching your face, especially your eyes, nose, and mouth. Cover your mouth and nose with a tissue or your elbow when coughing or sneezing.

5. Food and Water Safety: **Frankfurt is known for its culinary delights, but be cautious about food and water consumption. Drink bottled water or use a water purifier if necessary. Eat at reputable establishments and ensure that food is properly cooked and served hot.**

6. Personal Safety: **While Frankfurt is generally considered safe, take common-sense precautions. Be aware of your surroundings, particularly in crowded areas and public transportation. Keep your belongings secure and avoid displaying valuable items. Use trusted transportation services and be cautious of potential scams or pickpocketing.**

7. Emergency Contacts: **Save emergency contact numbers, including local authorities and your embassy or consulate, in your**

phone or write them down for quick access in case of any emergencies or unforeseen events.

Remember that health and safety considerations may evolve. Stay informed about current conditions and adapt your plans accordingly. By taking these precautions, you can enjoy your trip to Frankfurt while prioritizing your well-being and that of others around you.

CHAPTER 6: UNDERSTANDING FOREIGN TRANSACTION FEES

Avoid Cell Phone Roaming Charges

Staying connected when going abroad is crucial in the connected world of today. But it's important to be aware of the possible dangers, such as mobile phone roaming fees, which may have a big influence on your spending. This paper tries to clarify roaming fees for mobile phones in Frankfurt, Germany, and provide suggestions for reducing expenses while maintaining connectivity.

When you use your phone beyond the range of your home network's coverage, cellular service providers will apply extra costs known as "roaming charges." It's essential to understand the roaming fees before visiting Frankfurt, a place recognized for its thriving tourist industry and strong economy, to prevent any unpleasant surprises.

Guidelines for Reducing Roaming Fees:

1. Consult your supplier: **Before leaving, get in touch with your cellphone service provider to learn about their roaming prices and rules. Ask about temporary local SIM card possibilities or available international roaming plans, which may provide more affordable alternatives.**

2. Wi-Fi Accessibility: **Take use of the Wi-Fi hotspots Frankfurt has to offer. You may utilize messaging applications or phones using internet-based services like Voice over Internet Protocol (VoIP) since many cafés,**

hotels, and public spaces have free or inexpensive Wi-Fi.

3. Disable Data Roaming: In your phone's settings, disable data roaming to prevent accidental data consumption. This stops push notifications, background updates, and other data-intensive processes that can result in unforeseen fees.

4. Download Offline Maps: Download offline maps of Frankfurt before your trip, or utilize specialized navigation programs that support offline use. As a result, using data connection while touring the city is less necessary.

5. Use texting and calling applications that need an internet connection: like WhatsApp, Skype, or Viber. These applications utilize Wi-Fi or mobile data instead of the customary roaming fees.

6. Buy a Local SIM Card: **If you're going to be in Frankfurt for a lengthy amount of time or you'll need a lot of mobile data, you may want to buy a local SIM card. You may take advantage of local rates and avoid roaming fees with this choice.**

7. Be Aware of Roaming Zones: **Know the exact nations or areas that your roaming plan covers. Some service providers may include adjacent nations in their roaming coverage areas, enabling you to use your phone without paying additional fees.**

It's critical to comprehend mobile phone roaming fees while traveling to Frankfurt or any other foreign location. You may reduce the effect of roaming fees and remain connected without breaking the bank by being informed of your provider's restrictions, using Wi-Fi hotspots, turning off data roaming, and researching alternate communication options. Plan prepared, keep informed, and have fun when visiting Frankfurt without getting any nasty surprises on your cell account.

Consider a Frankfurt SIM Card or Mifi Device

Staying connected when traveling is crucial in the digital era, and Frankfurt, Germany's thriving financial center, is no exception. SIM cards and MiFi devices are two well-liked methods of preserving constant connection. This essay examines the value and benefits of these tools in Frankfurt, allowing visitors to easily traverse the city.

a SIM card

An embedded chip called a SIM (Subscriber Identity Module) card enables a mobile device to connect to a cellular network. Due to Frankfurt's outstanding network coverage, SIM cards are the best option for tourists. They provide various advantages:

1. Cost-Effective Communication: Travelers may avoid expensive roaming fees by getting a local SIM card in Frankfurt. Widely accessible prepaid SIM cards enable consumers to manage their spending and only pay for the services they use.

2. Seamless Connectivity: With a local SIM card, tourists may use their cellphones to connect to high-speed internet and keep in touch with friends, family, and necessary

services. When booking bookings or exploring the city, this connection comes in quite handy.

3. Local Services and Offers: Numerous local service providers provide SIM card customers access to special packages and offers. These packages often include significant data allotments and cheap call and text rates, further boosting the value for travelers.

MiFi gadgets

Mobile Wi-Fi hotspots, commonly referred to as MiFi devices are small, portable routers that link to cellular networks to build local Wi-Fi networks. In Frankfurt, MiFi devices have special benefits:

1. Multiple Device Connectivity: MiFi devices enable simultaneous connections

between several devices, including laptops, tablets, and smartphones. For group travelers or business people who want an internet connection on many devices, this capability is very helpful.

2. Flexibility and Convenience: MiFi products are small, light, and easily tucked away in a pocket or backpack. They provide mobility flexibility by enabling users to access the internet while on the move, whether they are traveling or attending meetings.

3. Secure Connection: MiFi devices provide a private and secure Wi-Fi connection, safeguarding confidential information and guaranteeing secure surfing. Travelers who often use free public Wi-Fi networks, which might be exposed to online attacks, should pay particular attention to this element.

Both SIM cards and MiFi gadgets are essential for keeping tourists connected in Frankfurt. These tools offer seamless connection, enabling tourists to explore the city, converse with locals, and access necessary internet services. They may be either the adaptability and convenience of a MiFi device or the affordable communication of a local SIM card. Travelers may make the most of their stay in Frankfurt by using these tools, assuring a seamless and connected experience.

Consider The Adapter and Converter

When traveling to Frankfurt, Germany, it is essential to be prepared with the necessary electrical adapters and converters to ensure that your electronic devices can be used safely and effectively. Frankfurt, like the rest of Germany, operates on a 230-volt electrical system with Type C and Type F outlets.

Type C outlets are the standard European two-pin plugs, while Type F outlets are the Schuko plugs with two pins and an additional grounding clip. These outlets may differ from the ones used in your home country, so having the right adapters and converters is crucial.

An adapter is a device that allows you to plug your electronic devices into different types of outlets. In Frankfurt, you will primarily need an adapter for Type C and Type F outlets. It is important to note that adapters only change the physical shape of the plug and do not convert the voltage. Therefore, if your devices are not compatible with 230 volts, you will also need a voltage converter.

A voltage converter, on the other hand, is designed to change the voltage of your devices. For example, if your devices are designed for the 120-volt system used in the United States, a voltage converter can step down the voltage from 230 volts to 120 volts. This is particularly important for appliances like hairdryers, curling irons, or certain types of chargers that are not dual voltage.

To ensure a smooth experience in Frankfurt, it is advisable to invest in a universal adapter and converter kit. These kits usually come with multiple adapters for various countries, including Germany. Additionally, they often include voltage converters that allow you to switch between different voltage settings. Make sure to check the wattage and voltage specifications of your devices before selecting an appropriate converter.

It is worth noting that many modern electronic devices, such as laptops, smartphones, and camera chargers, are already compatible with a wide range of voltages (typically 100-240 volts). In such cases, you may only need a simple adapter to plug them into the German outlets.

Before your trip, it is recommended to check with your accommodation if they provide adapters or converters for guest use. Some hotels may offer them upon request, saving you the trouble of purchasing or carrying your own.

When visiting Frankfurt, it is crucial to have the correct adapters and converters to ensure the safe and efficient use of your electronic devices. Investing in a universal adapter and converter kit will help you stay connected and avoid any potential issues with voltage compatibility during your stay in this vibrant German city.

Download Offline Map

Do you have travel plans to Frankfurt, Germany? Having access to trustworthy maps is essential whether you are a seasoned traveler or setting off on your first overseas excursion. Even though internet maps are now commonplace, having offline maps close at hand is still crucial. This essay examines the need for offline maps when traveling to Frankfurt and underlines the benefits they provide.

1. Unreliable or Sporadic Internet Connectivity: Despite Frankfurt's great internet infrastructure and contemporary cityscape, depending only on online maps may not always be safe. Subways, isolated communities, and busy tourist destinations are examples of places that could have a poor or nonexistent internet connection. You may travel without difficulty even in areas with limited internet by downloading

offline maps to your smartphone, ensuring you never get lost.

2. Cost savings: Using internet maps uses data, and when going overseas, roaming fees may add up rapidly. You may lessen your dependency on data roaming and save money by using offline maps. By using this economic strategy, you may spend more money on other travel-related activities, including trying the local food or seeing the sights.

3. Battery conservation: Taking in Frankfurt's dynamic culture necessitates using your mobile device often for a variety of tasks. Continually using internet maps will rapidly deplete your battery. On the other hand, offline maps use far less power, allowing you to save your device's battery life for other crucial tasks like recording

memories or keeping in touch with loved ones.

4. Instant Access: Without an internet connection, you get immediate access to important information when using offline maps. You may use the map at any moment, to find out where you are, plot out itineraries, and investigate sites of interest. When you need to discover something quickly, are having trouble connecting to the internet, or are attempting to find a certain place, this convenience is extremely helpful.

5. Increased Privacy and Security: While internet maps provide many benefits, there are also possible privacy issues. By using offline maps, you may rely less on outside applications, protecting the privacy of your movements and position. An experience of travel that is more comfortable and

worry-free might result from increased privacy and security.

Having offline maps accessible is a wise choice when planning a trip to Frankfurt. They provide accurate navigation, financial savings, battery conservation, immediate accessibility, and increased privacy. You may confidently traverse the city, discover hidden treasures, and make lifelong memories while guaranteeing a smooth and stress-free vacation experience by using offline maps. Therefore, to improve your journey, download offline maps before you go on your Frankfurt tour.

Learn Basic Language

There are a few languages that may significantly improve your experience and communication skills if you're traveling to Frankfurt, Germany. Frankfurt's official language is German, however, knowing a few other languages may be useful in a variety of contexts. The following three tongues might be useful throughout your visit:

1. German: Being familiar with German, Frankfurt's predominant language, would surely be helpful. Even though many residents, particularly in tourist locations, understand English, learning a few basic German words would demonstrate respect for the local way of life and make interactions more pleasant. You may also order food, use the transit system, and have regular chats with inhabitants with the aid of it.

2. English: **Although German is commonly
spoken in Frankfurt, English is also widely
understood there, especially in the city's
economic and tourism sections. The
majority of personnel in the hospitality
business, including those working in
restaurants and hotels, will speak English
well. However, it's always nice to pick up a
few German slang terms and try to converse
in the native tongue.**

3. Frankfurt is a multicultural metropolis
that draws tourists from across the world.
France is a country where many people
speak French. When dealing with locals or
guests who speak French, engaging in
discussion, or participating in cultural
activities, learning a few French words
might be helpful.

Frankfurt is also noteworthy for being a multicultural city with a sizable immigrant population. As a result, separate towns or neighborhoods could also be home to speakers of other languages including Turkish, Russian, Arabic, and Polish. Even while it would not be realistic to master every language spoken in Frankfurt, having an open mind and appreciation for all cultures and languages can make traveling more enjoyable.

Remember that even the most fundamental language abilities may help you communicate with individuals you encounter along the road, bridge cultural divides, and demonstrate your admiration for the local way of life. Having a working knowledge of a few essential words in the aforementioned languages can help you get by and make your vacation to Frankfurt memorable.

CHAPTER 7: CASH AND CREDIT CARD

Cash at the Airport is Expensive

Frankfurt Airport, one of the busiest and most prominent international airports in the world, offers a range of services to cater to the needs of its diverse travelers. While digital payment methods have gained popularity, having access to cash remains essential for certain transactions. This note examines the availability of cash at Frankfurt Airport, ensuring travelers are well-informed about their options.

Cash Dispensing Facilities:

Frankfurt Airport recognizes the importance of cash and provides several convenient options for travelers to access it. Numerous

ATMs are strategically located throughout the airport terminals, ensuring easy access for passengers. These ATMs, operated by well-known banks and financial institutions, allow travelers to withdraw cash in various currencies, including euros, US dollars, and British pounds, among others. Most ATMs accept major credit and debit cards, making it convenient for international travelers to obtain local currency.

Currency Exchange Services:

In addition to ATMs, Frankfurt Airport offers multiple currency exchange offices where travelers can convert their foreign currency into euros or other desired currencies. These offices are typically located in the arrival and departure areas of the airport and are easily recognizable by their signage. These currency exchange services provide competitive exchange rates and can accommodate various currencies, allowing travelers to obtain the required cash for their immediate needs.

Pre-Ordering Cash:

To enhance convenience and ensure availability, some currency exchange services at Frankfurt Airport offer the option of pre-ordering cash. Travelers can visit the websites of these providers in advance, select their desired currency and amount, and schedule a pickup at the airport. This service helps save time and ensures travelers have the required cash upon their arrival.

Frankfurt Airport recognizes the importance of cash and provides convenient options for travelers to access it. Whether through ATMs, currency exchange offices, or pre-ordering services, passengers can easily obtain the desired currency for their transactions. This availability ensures that travelers have the flexibility and convenience they need while passing through Frankfurt Airport.

Set up Apple pay or Google pay as an Option

Carrying cash in the current age of digital transactions is becoming less and less essential. Digital payment methods, such as Apple Pay and Google Pay, provide a more practical and secure option for your financial requirements. Using these mobile payment options may improve your travel experience, regardless of whether you're planning a vacation to Frankfurt, the financial center of Germany, or checking out the city's dynamic culture. We will discuss the advantages of Apple Pay and Google Pay in this letter and how they may make your transactions in Frankfurt more convenient.

1. Contactless Payments: Google Pay and Apple Pay both provide convenient contactless payment methods. You may pay by holding your iPhone or Android phone close to a contactless payment terminal by simply connecting your credit or debit card to your smartphone. You may pay quickly and easily using this option at many

restaurants, stores, and transit services in Frankfurt.

2. Broad popularity: In several Frankfurt businesses, both Apple Pay and Google Pay have attained broad popularity. Many companies, from well-known retailers to neighborhood shops, now accept digital payments. This eliminates the need to carry several cards or convert currencies by allowing you to pay for meals, purchase rides on public transit, and other services using your mobile device.

3. Enhanced Security: By placing a high priority on security, Apple Pay and Google Pay are secure alternatives to physical cards. Your credit card information isn't sent to the business directly when you utilize these services. Instead, each transaction generates a special token that protects your private

data. Additionally, biometric identification techniques like Face ID or Touch ID give an added degree of protection by guaranteeing that only you have the authority to approve payments.

4. Currency Conversion: If you're coming from another nation to Frankfurt, currency conversion might be difficult. However, you may connect several cards, including those from international banks, with both Apple Pay and Google Pay. You may quickly make payments in the local currency using their integrated currency conversion capabilities, saving you time and perhaps paying foreign exchange costs.

5. Transaction History and Budgeting: Being able to keep track of your travel spending is one benefit of utilizing Apple Pay or Google Pay in Frankfurt. These systems provide you

access to a thorough transaction history that gives you a breakdown of your expenditure. While traveling the city, you may simply keep track of your spending, classify it, and maintain financial organization.

Having a trustworthy and secure payment option is essential while traveling to Frankfurt. A quick and easy method to manage your financial transactions while traveling is using Apple Pay or Google Pay. These mobile payment systems may expedite your experience and enable you to concentrate on taking advantage of all Frankfurt has to offer thanks to their contactless payment alternatives, broad acceptance, improved security features, currency conversion capabilities, and expenditure monitoring. Don't forget to use

Apple Pay or Google Pay to make payments as easy as possible while enjoying your Frankfurt journey.

CHAPTER 8: MAKING YOUR STAY ENJOYABLE IN FRANKFURT

Frankfurt Airports and Their Closest Hotel

Here are the two airports in Frankfurt and their closest hotels:

1. Frankfurt Airport (FRA): This is the main airport in Frankfurt and is located about 10 kilometers from the city center. Some of the closest hotels to Frankfurt Airport include:

- Hilton Garden Inn Frankfurt Airport

Hilton Garden Inn Frankfurt Airport

Image of Hilton Garden Inn Frankfurt Airport

- NH Hotel Frankfurt Airport

NH Hotel Frankfurt Airport

Image of NH Hotel Frankfurt Airport

- Holiday Inn Frankfurt Airport, an IHG Hotel

Holiday Inn Frankfurt Airport, an IHG Hotel

Image of Holiday Inn Frankfurt Airport, an IHG Hotel

- Moxy Frankfurt Airport

MOXY Frankfurt Airport

Image of Moxy Frankfurt Airport

2. Frankfurt Hahn Airport (HHN): This is a smaller airport in Frankfurt and is located about 120 kilometers from the city center. Some of the closest hotels to Frankfurt Hahn Airport include:

- ## Prizeotel Frankfurt Hahn

Image of Prizeotel Frankfurt Hahn

- ## Hotel Zur Krone

Image of Hotel Zur Krone

- Hotel am Airport

Image of Hotel am Airport

- Airport Hotel Hahn

Image of Airport Hotel Hahn

5 Low-cost Hotel Options

Below are 5 budget-friendly hotels in Frankfurt:

1. ibis cheap Frankfurt City Ost: A contemporary budget hotel with a vibrant eating area and inviting rooms decorated in a current style.

2. A&O Frankfurt Gallusware: **Budget hostel with free WiFi, gaming area, and both shared and private rooms available.**

3. Panorama Hostel Frankfurt: **Unpretentious rooms and dormitories at a hostel that offers breakfast, a common kitchen, and a bar.**

4. The Mainbogen Hotel: **Functional lodging with some balconies in a low-key building with a laid-back bar.**

5. Hotel Europa Life: **Location is convenient, and there are basic rooms with flat-screen TVs and complimentary Wi-Fi.**

There are several services available at these hotels, such as free WiFi, breakfast, and a bar or restaurant. They're all in handy locations, near to transit options and well-liked tourist destinations.

5 Luxurious Places to Stay

Here are 5 luxurious places to stay in
Frankfurt:

1. The Westin Grand Frankfurt: **This 5-star**
hotel is located in the heart of Frankfurt,
just steps from the Main River. It features a
spa, a fitness center, and a rooftop terrace
with stunning views of the city.

2. Steigenberger Frankfurter Hof: **This**
iconic hotel has been welcoming guests
since 1876. It is located in the city center,
near the Opera House and the Römerberg.
The hotel has a spa, a fitness center, and 3
restaurants.

3. Sofitel Frankfurt Opera: **This 5-star hotel**
is located in the heart of Frankfurt, just
steps from the Opera House. It features a

spa, a fitness center, and a rooftop terrace with stunning views of the city.

4. Roomers: This boutique hotel is located in the trendy district of Sachsenhausen. It features a spa, a fitness center, and a rooftop terrace with views of the city.

5. The Ritz-Carlton, Frankfurt: This 5-star hotel is located in the heart of Frankfurt, near the Main River. It features a spa, a fitness center, and a rooftop terrace with stunning views of the city.

These hotels offer a variety of amenities, including luxurious accommodations, excellent service, and convenient locations. They are all perfect for a special occasion or a luxurious getaway.

3 Days Frankfurt Itinerary

For your trip to Frankfurt, here is a proposed 3-day itinerary:

Day 1:

Morning: 1. Begin your day by seeing Frankfurt's "Altstadt," the city's historic core. Discover Frankfurt's City Hall, the renowned Römer building, and other attractive half-timbered homes in the Römerberg plaza.

2. Enjoy the stunning scenery by taking a walk along the River Main. A pedestrian bridge with love locks is the Eiserner Steg, which you can also visit.

3. Visit the Museumsufer (Museum Embankment), a region along the Main River that is home to several top-notch institutions. Depending on your interests, you may decide to visit a few museums, such as the German Film Museum, the Museum of Modern Art (MMK), or the Städel Museum (an art museum).

4. Have a short meal at a nearby café or eatery. Bratwurst and schnitzel are two typical German delicacies that you shouldn't pass up.

Evening: 5. Visit Sachsenhausen, known for its authentic cider pubs (Apfelweinlokale). Enjoy the typical Frankfurt food and the local apple wine. You may also enjoy the vibrant ambiance by going to a classic apple wine tavern.

Day 2:

Morning: 1. Begin your day by seeing Frankfurt's Palmengarten, a stunning botanical park. Enjoy the peace by taking a leisurely walk around the numerous themed gardens.

2. Visit the beautiful Gothic-style cathedral known as the Frankfurt Cathedral (Frankfurter Dom). Atop the tower, you may get a bird's-eye perspective of the city.

3. Visit Frankfurt's largest shopping district, the Zeil, where you may discover a variety of retailers, department stores, and boutiques.

Investigate the numerous retail malls, such as MyZeil and Zeilgalerie.

4. The Staufermauer (Staufen Wall), the remains of the medieval city wall, and the Archaeological Garden, which highlights the Roman heritage of the city, are also worthwhile historical stops.

Evening: 5. Check out Bornheim or Nordend to see Frankfurt's exciting nightlife. The hip bars, inviting pubs, and live music venues in these districts are well-known.

Day 3:

Morning: 1. Go on a day excursion to the quaint town of Heidelberg nearby, which is renowned for its magnificent castle and ancient Old Town. Train travel from

Frankfurt takes roughly an hour. Discover the castle grounds, stroll down Philosopher's Walk for panoramic views, and explore the Old Town's narrow lanes.

Afternoon: 2. Visit the Goethe House in Frankfurt once again. This was the previous home of famed German author Johann Wolfgang von Goethe. The displays and artifacts on display will teach you about his life and creative endeavors.

3. Check out the Commerzbank Tower or the Frankfurt Trade Fair Tower (Messeturm), two recognizable buildings that dominate the city's skyline, if you're interested in contemporary architecture.

4. In the evening, take a leisurely dinner boat along the River Main to round off your journey. While enjoying a great lunch on board, take in the sights of Frankfurt's lit skyline.

Keep in mind to modify the schedule to account for your interests, attraction opening times, and any special events or exhibitions taking place while you are there.

7 Days Frankfurt Itinerary

Day 1: Arrival and City Exploration

Upon arrival in Frankfurt, settle into your accommodation and start your adventure in this vibrant city. Begin by exploring the historic city center, Altstadt, where you'll find attractions like Römerberg, the city's old town square, and the iconic Romer, a medieval building complex. Take a stroll along the Main River and visit the Frankfurt Cathedral, known as Dom St. Bartholomaus, which offers stunning views from its tower. End your day with a visit to the Museum Embankment, home to several world-class museums.

Day 2: Day Trip to Heidelberg

Take a day trip to Heidelberg, a charming town located about an hour away from Frankfurt. Explore the magnificent Heidelberg Castle, perched on a hill overlooking the city. Visit the historic Old Town, wander along the picturesque streets, and enjoy the baroque-style architecture. Don't forget to walk across the iconic Old Bridge, adorned with beautiful sculptures. In the evening, return to Frankfurt and unwind by exploring its lively nightlife scene.

Day 3: Modern Frankfurt

Discover the modern side of Frankfurt on day three. Begin with a visit to the Frankfurt Skyline Plaza, a shopping center with an observation deck that offers panoramic views of the city. Explore the futuristic European Central Bank, the financial district, and the Main Tower, which provides another fantastic viewpoint. Indulge in some retail therapy on the famous Zeil shopping street or visit the Palmengarten, a stunning botanical garden.

Day 4: Day Trip to Rhine Valley

Embark on a scenic day trip to the Rhine Valley, known for its picturesque landscapes and charming villages. Take a boat tour along the Rhine River, passing by vineyards, medieval castles, and the legendary Lorelei Rock. Explore towns like Rüdesheim and Bacharach, known for their half-timbered houses and wine production. Enjoy a wine tasting experience and savor the local cuisine before returning to Frankfurt.

Day 5: Museums and Galleries

Dedicate day five to Frankfurt's rich cultural scene. Start with a visit to the Städel Museum, one of Germany's most important art museums, showcasing works from the Middle Ages to contemporary art. Explore the Museum of Modern Art (MMK) and the Senckenberg Natural History Museum. In the evening, enjoy a performance at the Alte Oper, a grand concert hall that hosts classical music concerts and other cultural events.

Day 6: Frankfurt Green Spaces

Escape the bustling city and spend the day in Frankfurt's green spaces. Visit the Frankfurt City Forest, a vast woodland area perfect for hiking or cycling. Explore the Palmengarten, a botanical garden with a wide variety of plant species. Take a relaxing stroll in the Nizza Park or enjoy a picnic in the Stadtwald Park. In the evening, experience the local cuisine at one of Frankfurt's traditional apple wine taverns.

Day 7: Departure

On your last day, take the opportunity to revisit any favorite spots or explore any missed attractions in Frankfurt. Visit the

Kleinmarkthalle, a bustling food market, to taste local specialties and buy souvenirs. Take a final walk along the riverbanks or indulge in some last-minute shopping. Bid farewell to Frankfurt as you depart for your next destination, filled with lasting memories of your time in this diverse and dynamic city.

Top 5 Events to Attend in Frankfurt

Here are the top 5 events to attend in Frankfurt:

1. Frankfurt Book Fair: This is the world's largest book fair, and it takes place every year in October. It is a great place to see new books, meet authors, and learn about the latest trends in publishing.

2. Volksfest: This is a traditional German festival that takes place every year in

September. It features rides, games, food, and beer.

3. Frankfurt Christmas Markets: **These markets are open from late November to December, and they are a great place to buy Christmas gifts, Christmas decorations, and traditional German food.**

4. Jazz Festival Frankfurt: **This festival takes place every year in July, and it features a variety of jazz musicians from all over the world.**

5. Mainhattan Festival: **This festival takes place every year in June, and it features a variety of music, art, and food.**

These are just a few of the many events that take place in Frankfurt throughout the year. There is something for everyone, so be sure to check out the event calendar before you visit.

CHAPTER 9:DOs AND DON'Ts FOR TOURISTS

Saving Money Tips

Frankfurt offers a wealth of attractions and experiences. However, it's no secret that city exploration can put a strain on your wallet. To help you make the most of your visit without breaking the bank, here are some valuable money-saving tips for navigating Frankfurt.

1. Plan your visit during off-peak seasons:

Consider visiting Frankfurt during the shoulder seasons (spring and autumn) when the weather is pleasant, and tourist crowds are thinner. Accommodation and flight prices tend to be more affordable during these times, allowing you to save money on your overall travel expenses.

2. Opt for budget-friendly accommodation: Frankfurt boasts a range of accommodation options suitable for various budgets. Look for budget hotels, hostels, or guesthouses in the city center or slightly outside. Booking in advance and utilizing travel comparison websites can help you find the best deals and save significant amounts on your accommodation costs.

3. Utilize public transportation: Frankfurt has an efficient and well-connected public transportation system, including buses, trams, and trains. Purchase a day pass or a multi-day ticket to enjoy unlimited travel within the city. Public transportation is not only cost-effective but also offers the added benefit of convenience, allowing you to

explore Frankfurt's top attractions without the hassle of parking or navigating traffic.

4. Take advantage of free attractions: Frankfurt offers several free attractions and activities that allow you to experience the city's culture and history without spending a dime. Explore the picturesque Römerberg Square, visit the stunning St. Bartholomew's Cathedral, or take a stroll along the Main River promenade. Additionally, many museums offer free admission on specific days or during certain hours, so plan your visits accordingly.

5. Pack your meals or explore affordable dining options: Eating out can be one of the biggest expenses while traveling. To save money, consider packing your meals or snacks for day trips. Frankfurt's grocery stores and markets offer a variety of fresh

and affordable produce. When dining out, explore local eateries, street food vendors, or affordable restaurants serving traditional German cuisine. This way, you can experience the local flavors without draining your wallet.

6. Look for discounted tickets and city passes: Keep an eye out for discounted tickets and city passes that offer bundled deals on popular attractions, public transportation, and even discounts at local restaurants and shops. These passes can provide substantial savings, especially if you plan to visit multiple attractions.

7. Shop smartly: If you enjoy shopping, consider visiting Zeil, Frankfurt's main shopping street, where you can find a range of shops catering to different budgets. Look for discounts, sales, or outlet stores for

additional savings. Additionally, take advantage of the city's VAT refund program for non-European Union residents, which allows you to claim back a portion of the Value Added Tax (VAT) on eligible purchases.

Exploring Frankfurt on a budget is entirely possible with some planning and savvy decision-making. By following these money-saving tips, you can enjoy all that Frankfurt has to offer without putting a strain on your wallet. Remember to prioritize experiences and immerse yourself in the rich culture and history of this fascinating city while keeping your expenses in check.

FAQ

In what region is Frankfurt?

Frankfurt is situated in the Hesse region of central Germany. It is located along the Main River's banks.

What has Frankfurt become famous for?

Frankfurt has several reputations. The European Central Bank and the Frankfurt Stock Exchange are located there, making it a significant financial hub. Additionally well-known is its contemporary skyline, which gave rise to the moniker "Manhattan." Frankfurt is also well-known for its yearly trade fairs, such as the Frankfurt Book Fair, and for being Johann Wolfgang von Goethe's historical birthplace.

How do I go to Frankfurt?

Frankfurt is well-connected and simple to get there via a variety of transportation options. Frankfurt Airport (FRA), one of the busiest airports in Europe, is a significant international airport serving the city. It provides flights to locations all over the globe and acts as a hub for many carriers. With frequent train links to other German cities and nearby nations, Frankfurt is also a significant rail hub.

What are some of Frankfurt's well-liked tourism destinations?

A few of Frankfurt's well-liked tourist attractions are as follows:

- The Römerberg, a historic plaza with magnificently preserved half-timbered houses in the heart of the city.

Frankfurt church, also known as the Kaiserdom, is a Gothic-style church with an observation platform that provides sweeping vistas of the city.

- Städel Museum: One of Germany's top art institutions, it is home to a sizable collection of European works of art.

- Palmengarten: A botanical garden with several themed sections and a sizable network of greenhouses.

- Main Tower: A tower with a viewing platform that offers breathtaking views of the metropolis.

- Goethe House, the great author Johann Wolfgang von Goethe's birthplace is now a museum.

Is it safe to go to Frankfurt?

In general, Frankfurt is a safe place to visit, but like with any significant metropolitan region, it is wise to exercise care. Be cautious in tourist hotspots, watch your possessions, and be aware of your surroundings, especially in crowded locations and on public transit. Consult travel advisories and adhere to any local laws or regulations wherever possible.

What time of year is ideal for visiting Frankfurt?

The seasons of spring (April to June) and fall (September to October), when the weather is moderate and pleasant, are the greatest times to visit Frankfurt. These times of year provide pleasant weather for taking in the city's sights and engaging in outdoor activities. The attractions of Frankfurt are open all year round, even though summers may be pretty warm and winters can get quite cold.

Are English speakers in Frankfurt well-understood?

The majority of people in Frankfurt can communicate in English, notably at tourist attractions, lodging facilities, dining establishments, and retail establishments. Many residents speak English well, especially those who work in the tourist and service sectors. However, to improve communication and demonstrate respect for the local culture, it's always beneficial to learn a few fundamental German words or carry a translation tool.

What is the regional food in Frankfurt?

Frankfurt is renowned for its regional cuisine, which features classic dishes like "Frankfurter Würstchen" (a type of sausage frequently served with mustard and bread rolls) and "Frankfurter Grüne Sauce" (green sauce made with herbs and sour cream, typically served with boiled potatoes and hard-boiled eggs). Other area delicacies include the apple wine known as "Ebbelwoi" and "Handkäse mit Musik," a sort of sour milk cheese with onions and vinegar dressing.

Can I leave Frankfurt for a day trip?

Frankfurt is a great place to start day visits to adjacent locations because of its central position. Among the most popular choices are: - Heidelberg:

Conclusion

Frankfurt is a vibrant and diverse city that offers a unique blend of history, culture, and modernity. As one of Germany's major financial and business centers, it boasts an impressive skyline dominated by towering skyscrapers. However, beyond its corporate facade, Frankfurt has a rich and captivating heritage that is evident in its historic architecture, museums, and cultural institutions.

Visitors to Frankfurt are spoiled for choice when it comes to attractions and activities. The city's old town, known as Altstadt, is a charming area with narrow streets, picturesque squares, and beautifully restored buildings. The Römerberg square, with its iconic half-timbered houses, is a must-see, along with the stunning Frankfurt Cathedral. The city's diverse range of museums caters to all interests, from art enthusiasts at the Städel Museum to history buffs at the German Historical Museum.

One of the highlights of a visit to Frankfurt is the Palmengarten, a botanical garden that spans over 50 acres and showcases an incredible variety of plants from around the world. The surrounding green spaces, such as the Frankfurt City Forest and the Main Riverbanks, offer peaceful retreats for nature lovers and outdoor enthusiasts.

Frankfurt's culinary scene is also worth exploring, with a wide range of restaurants serving traditional German dishes as well as international cuisine. The local specialty, Apfelwein (apple wine), is a must-try, especially when paired with hearty regional dishes like sausages and sauerkraut.

Transportation in Frankfurt is efficient and convenient, with an extensive public transportation network that includes buses, trams, and trains. The city's central location within Germany makes it an ideal base for exploring other parts of the country, with easy access to destinations like Heidelberg, the Rhine Valley, and the Black Forest.

Frankfurt offers a captivating blend of history, culture, and modernity, making it a fascinating destination for travelers. Whether you're interested in exploring its rich history, immersing yourself in its thriving cultural scene, or simply enjoying its picturesque landscapes, Frankfurt has something to offer everyone. So, pack your bags, immerse yourself in the city's vibrant energy, and prepare for an unforgettable experience in the heart of Germany.

MAPS

Direction from Frankfurt Airport (FRA) to Hilton Garden Inn Frankfurt Airport

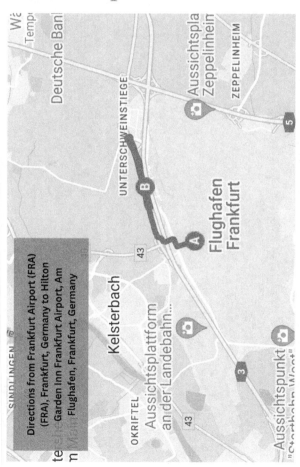

Direction From Frankfurt Hahn Airport (HHN) to Hotel Zur Krone

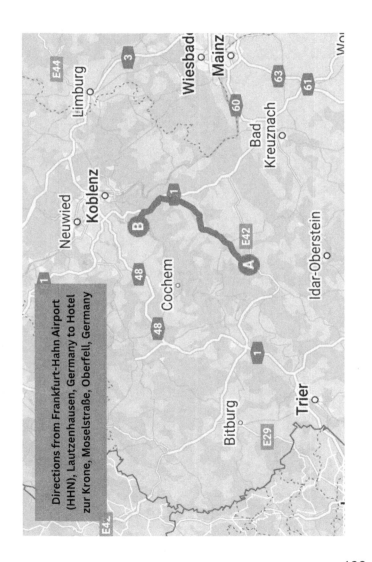

Directions from Frankfurt-Hahn Airport (HHN), Lautzenhausen, Germany to Hotel zur Krone, Moselstraße, Oberfell, Germany

Direction From Frankfurt Airport (FRA) to Panorama Hostel Frankfurt

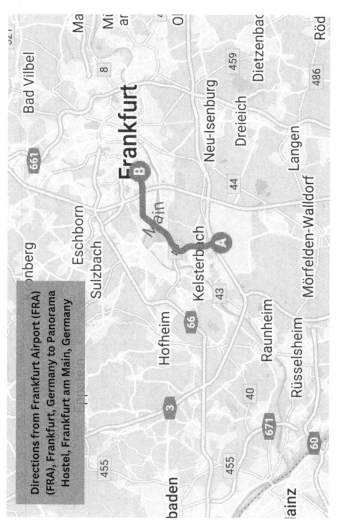

Directions from Frankfurt Airport (FRA) (FRA), Frankfurt, Germany to Panorama Hostel, Frankfurt am Main, Germany

Direction From Frankfurt Hahn Airport (HHN) to The Ritz-Carlton, FrankfurtSteigenberger Frankfurter Hof

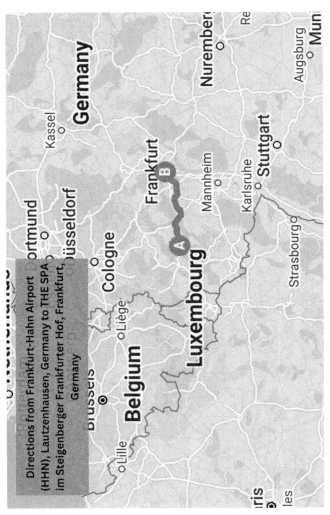

Directions from Frankfurt-Hahn Airport (HHN), Lautzenhausen, Germany to THE SPA im Steigenberger Frankfurter Hof, Frankfurt, Germany

185

Printed in Great Britain
by Amazon